FOR ORGANS, PIANOS & ELECTRONIC KEYBOARDS

E-Z PLAY TODAY

121

BOOGIES, BLUES & RAGS

E-Z Play TODAY chord notation is designed for playing **standard chord positions** or **single key chords** on all **major brand organs** and **portable keyboards**.

Contents

T0056534

2 Basin Street Blues
4 Boogie Woogie
20 Bugle Call Rag
8 Dallas Blues
42 Do You Know What It Means
 To Miss New Orleans
26 Entertainer, The
22 Good Man Is Hard To Find, A
14 Hard Hearted Hannah
32 Ivory Rag
28 King Porter Stomp
10 Livery Stable Blues
34 Man That Got Away, The
39 Maple Leaf Rag
16 Milenberg Joys
36 Pine Top's Boogie
18 Stormy Weather
30 Sugar Foot Stomp
6 Tin Roof Blues
24 Weary Blues
12 Wolverine Blues

44 Music Basics
46 Guitar Chord Chart
18 Chord Speller Chart (Keyboard)

HAL•LEONARD®
CORPORATION

7777 W. BLUEMOUND RD. P.O. BOX 13819 MILWAUKEE, WI 53213

Basin Street Blues

Registration 1
Rhythm: Swing or Fox Trot

By Spencer Williams

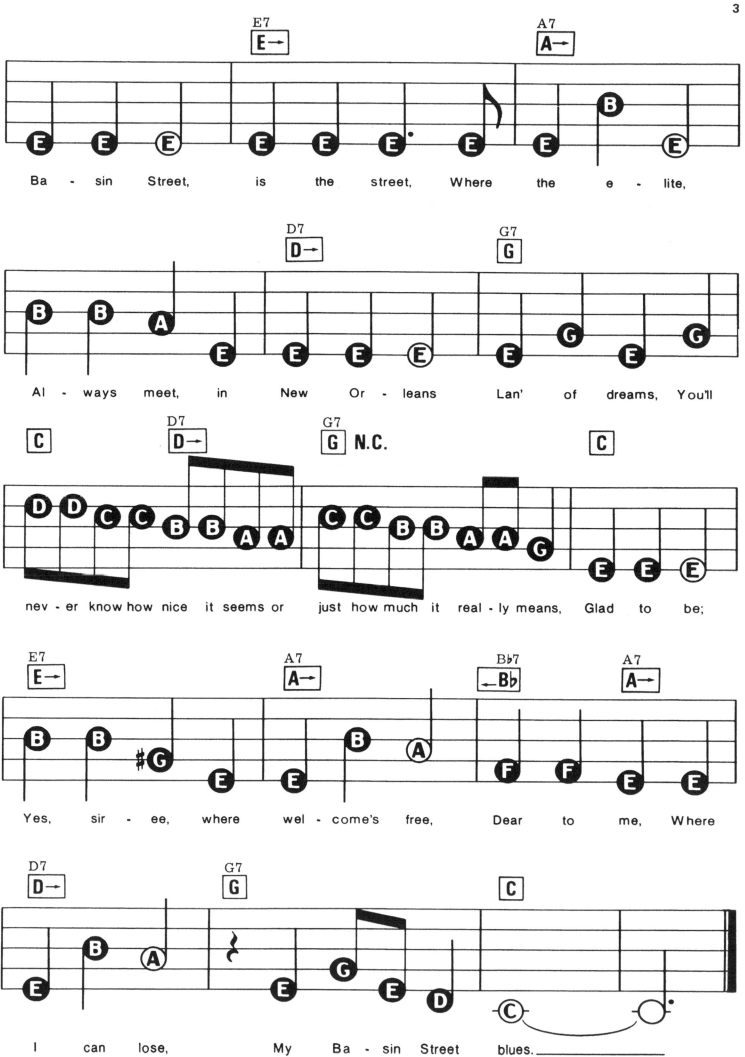

(The Original "Pine Top")
Boogie Woogie

Registration 8
Rhythm: Swing or Fox Trot

By Clarence "Pine Top" Smith

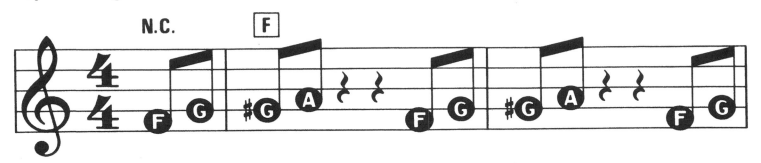

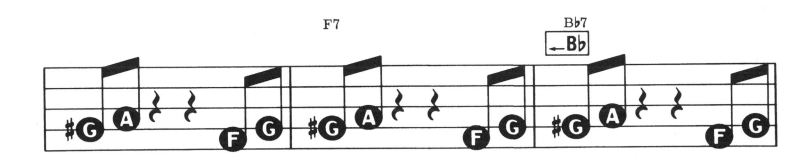

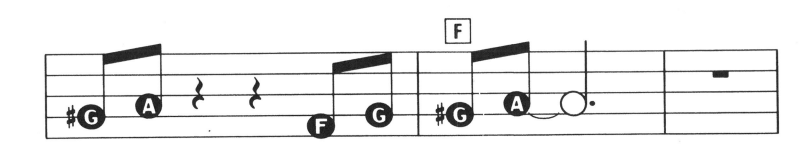

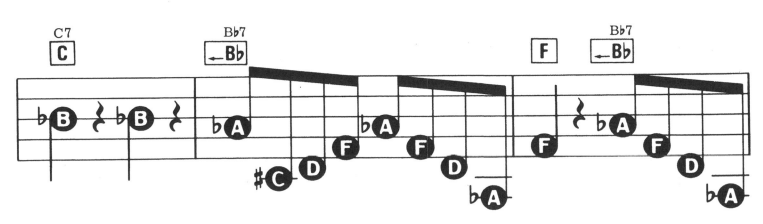

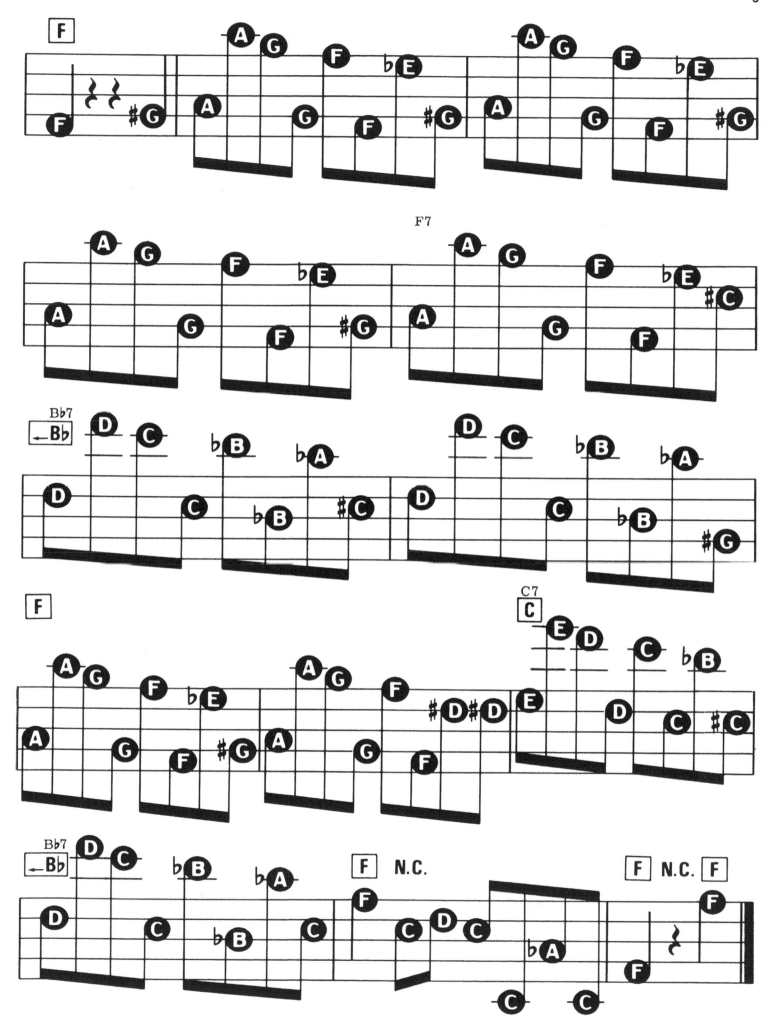

Tin Roof Blues

Registration 4
Rhythn: Ballad or Fox Trot

Lyric by Walter Melrose
Music by New Orleans Rhythm Kings

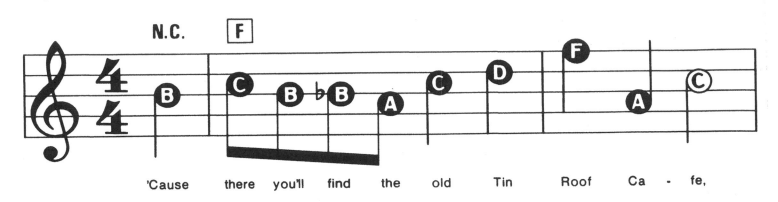

'Cause there you'll find the old Tin Roof Ca - fe,

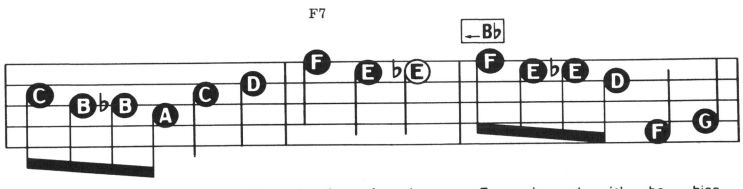

Where they play the blues till break of day, Fas - cin - at - in' ba - bies

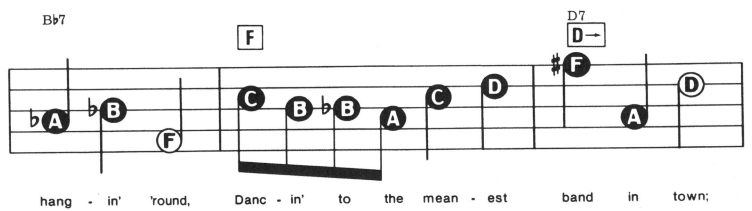

hang - in' 'round, Danc - in' to the mean - est band in town;

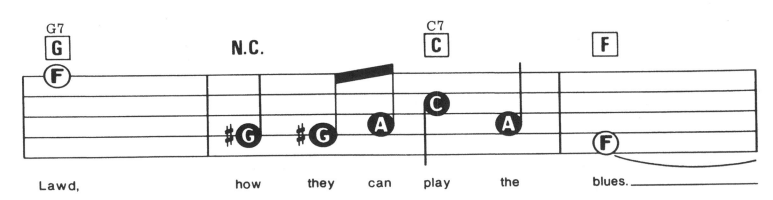

Lawd, how they can play the blues._____

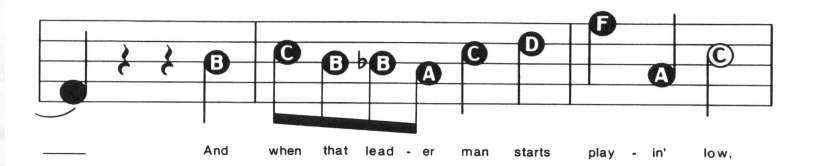

_____ And when that lead - er man starts play - in' low,

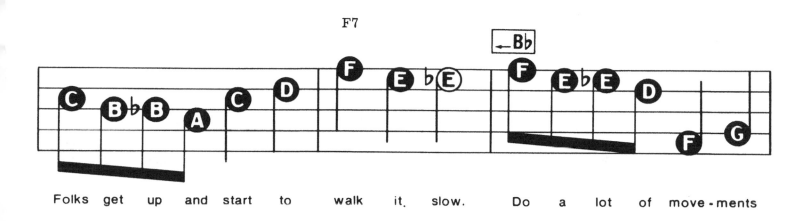

Folks get up and start to walk it. slow. Do a lot of move - ments

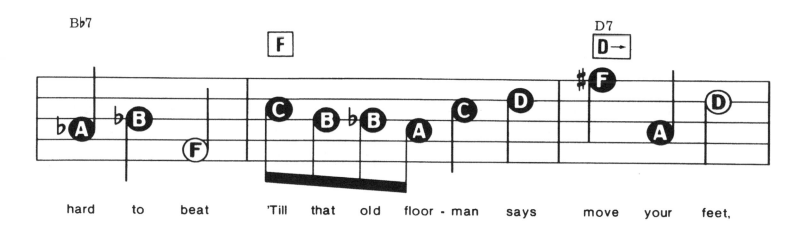

hard to beat 'Till that old floor - man says move your feet,

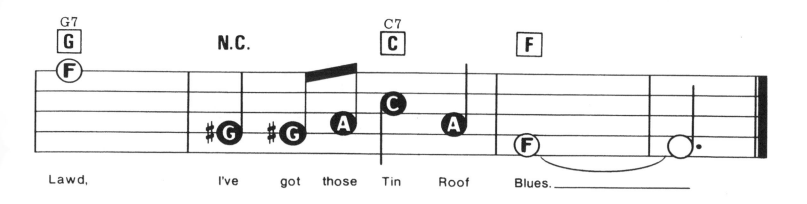

Lawd, I've got those Tin Roof Blues. _____

Dallas Blues

Registration 9
Rhythm: Ballad or Fox Trot

Lyric by Lloyd Garrett
Music by Hart A. Wand

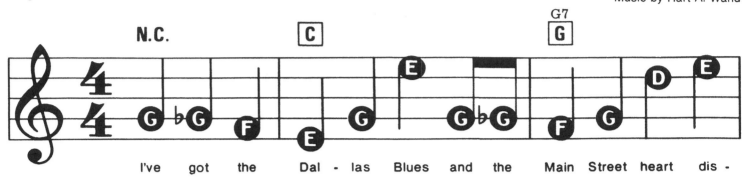

I've got the Dal - las Blues and the Main Street heart dis -

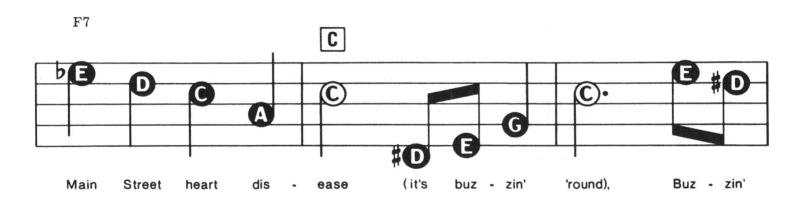

ease (it's buz - zin' 'round), I've got the Dal - las Blues and the

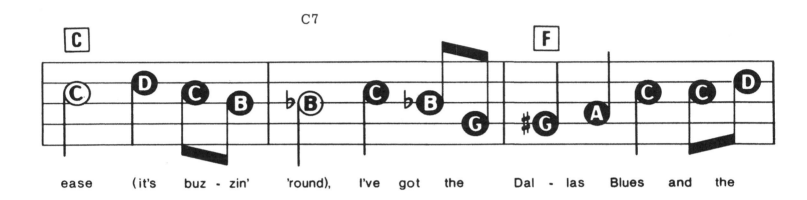

Main Street heart dis - ease (it's buz - zin' 'round), Buz - zin'

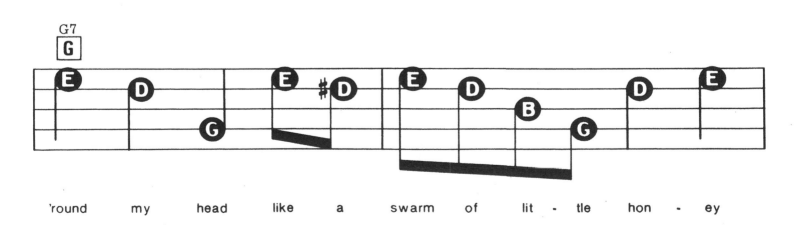

'round my head like a swarm of lit - tle hon - ey

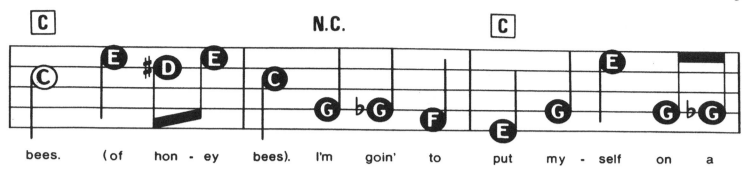

bees. (of hon - ey bees). I'm goin' to put my - self on a

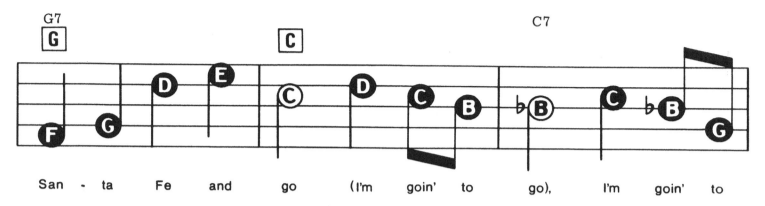

San - ta Fe and go (I'm goin' to go), I'm goin' to

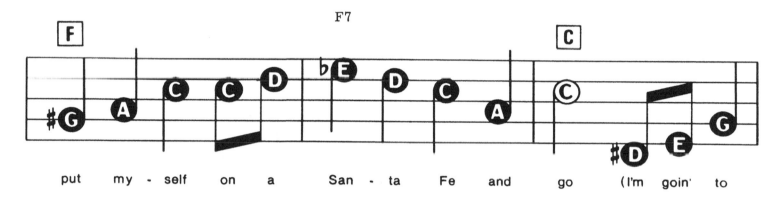

put my - self on a San - ta Fe and go (I'm goin' to

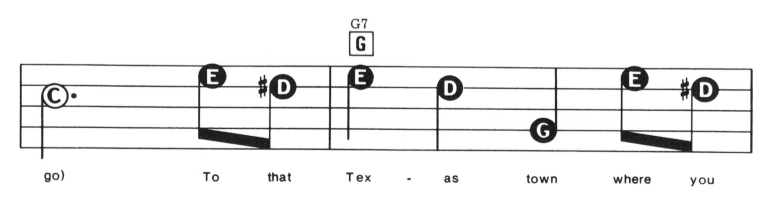

go) To that Tex - as town where you

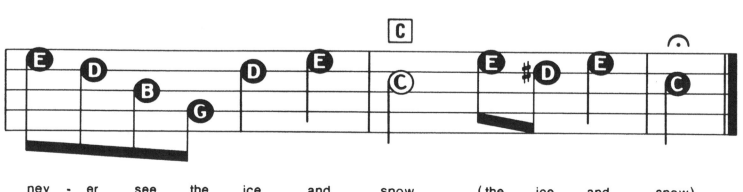

nev - er see the ice and snow (the ice and snow).

Live.y Stable Blu s
(Barnyard Blues)

Registration 2
Rhythm: Ballad or Fox Trot

Lyric by Marvin Lee
Music by Ray Lopez and Alcide Nunez

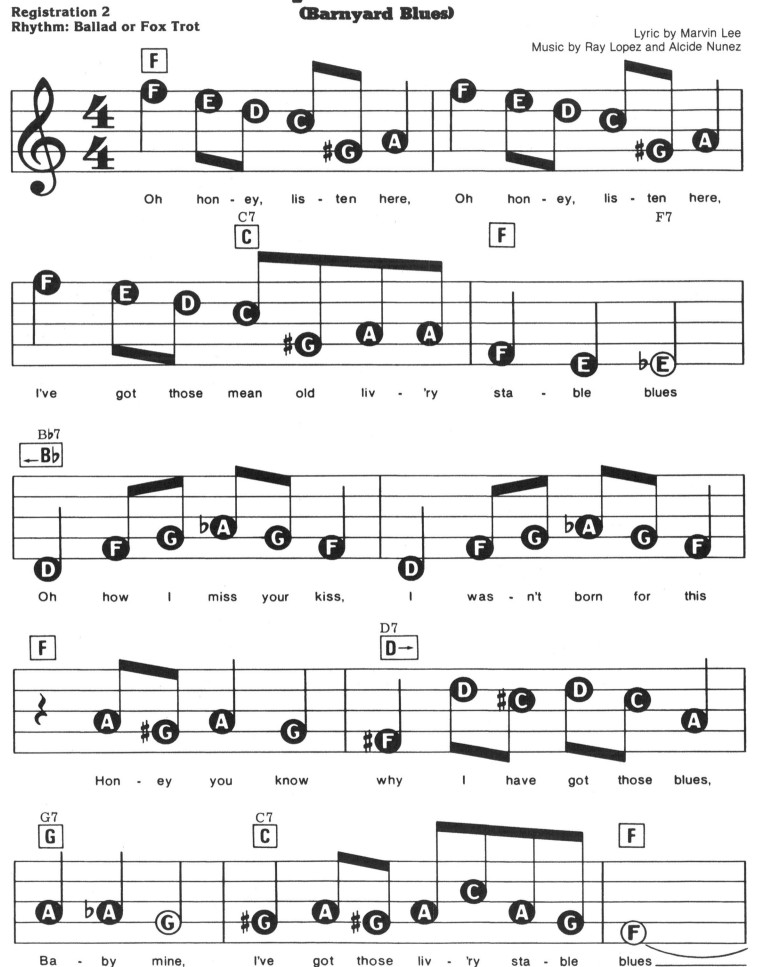

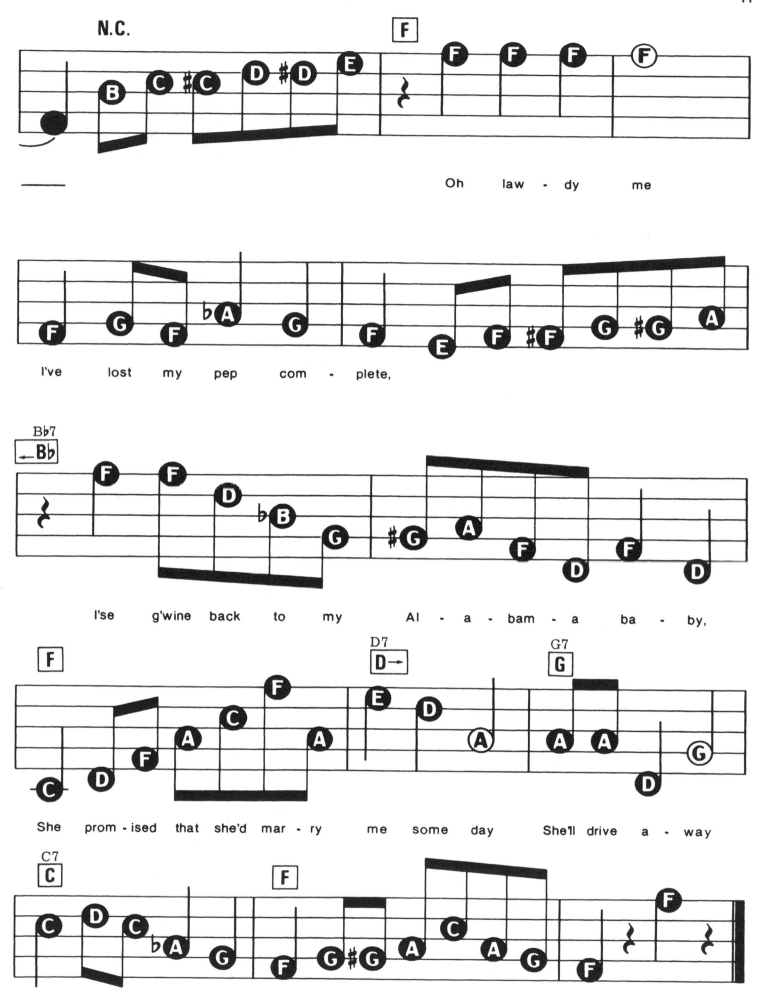

Wolverine Blues

Registration 3
Rhythm: Swing or Ballad

Lyric by John Spikes
and Benjamin Spikes
Music by Ferd Morton

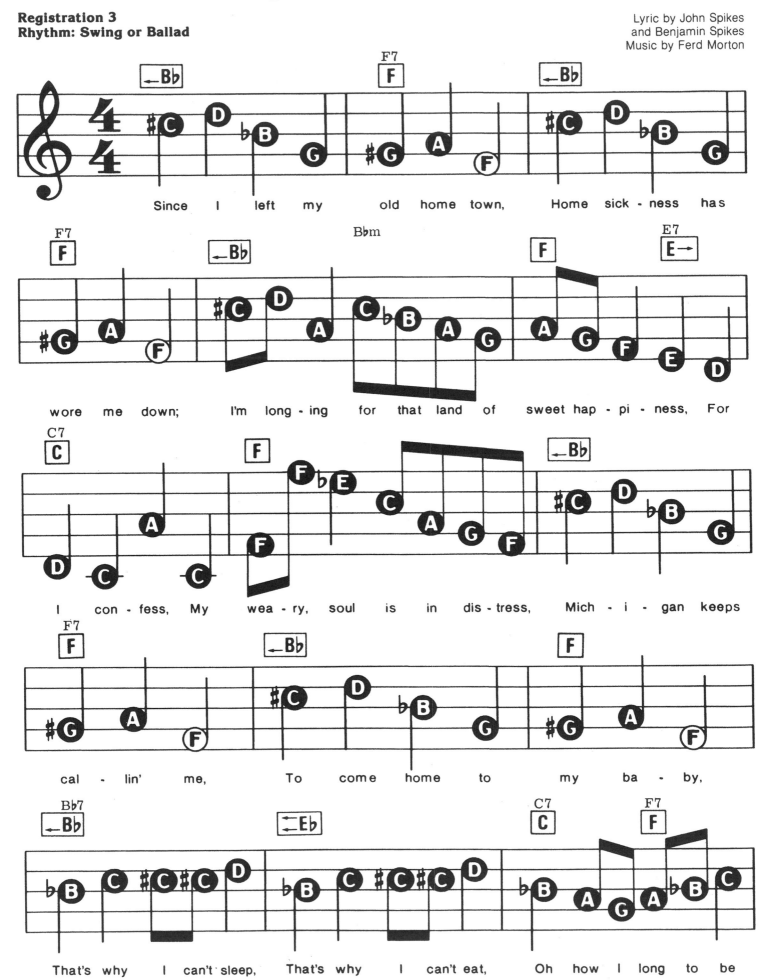

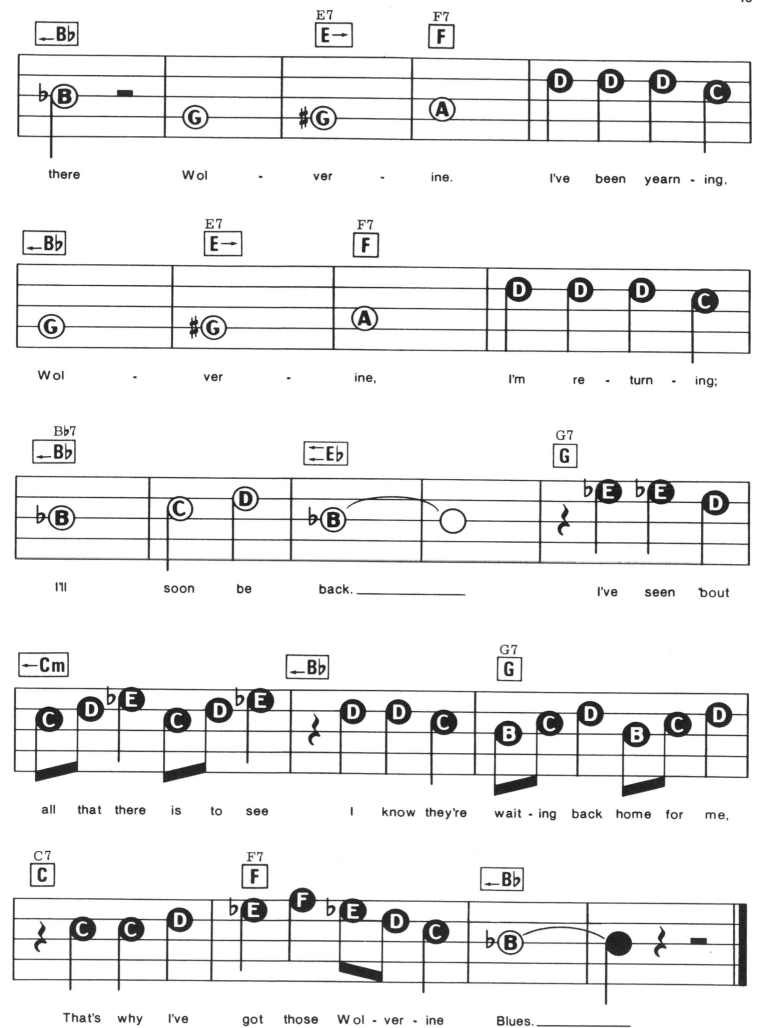

13

Hard Hearted Hannah
(The Vamp Of Savannah)

By Jack Yellen, Milton Ager,
Bob Bigelow, Chas Bates

Registration 2
Rhythm: Swing

They call her hard heart-ed Han-nah, the vamp of Sa-van-nah,
hard heart-ed Han-nah, the vamp of Sa-van-nah,

The mean-est gal in town; Leath-er is tough, but
The mean-est gal in town; Talk of your cold, re-

Han-nah's heart is tough-er; She's a gal who loves to
frig-er-at-ing Mam-mas, Broth-er, she's the Po-lar

see men suf-fer! To tease 'em and thrill 'em, To
bear's men pa-ja-mas! To tease 'em and thrill 'em To

Milenberg Joys

Registration 3
Rhythm: Swing or Ballad

Lyric by Walter Melrose
Music by Leon Roppolo, Paul Mares
and Jelly Roll Morton

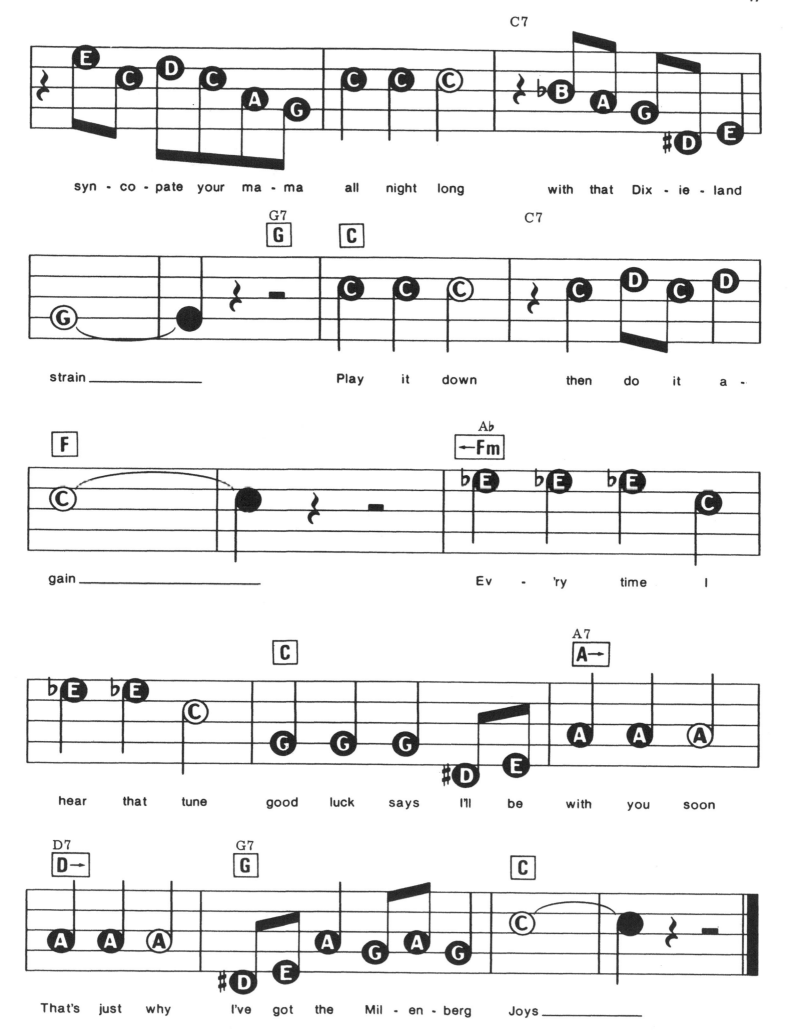

Stormy Weather
(Keeps Rainin' All The Time)

Lyric by Ted Koehler
Music by Harold Arlen

Registration 2
Rhythm: Ballad or Rhythm 'n' Blues

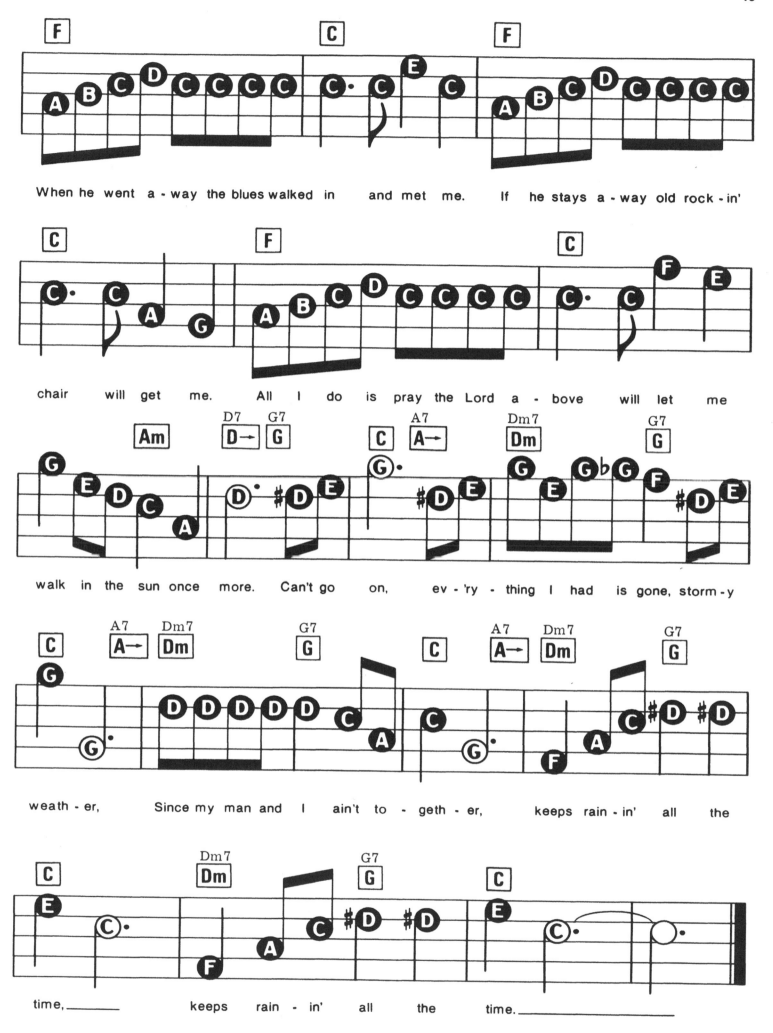

Bugle Call Rag

Registration 5
Rhythm: Rhythm 'n' Blues or Fox Trot

By Jack Pettis, Billy Meyers
and Elmer Schoebel

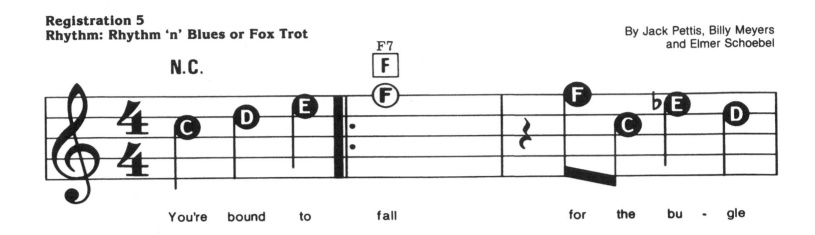

You're   bound   to   fall   for   the   bu - gle

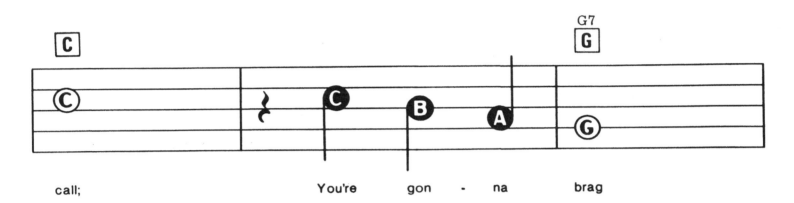

call;   You're   gon - na   brag

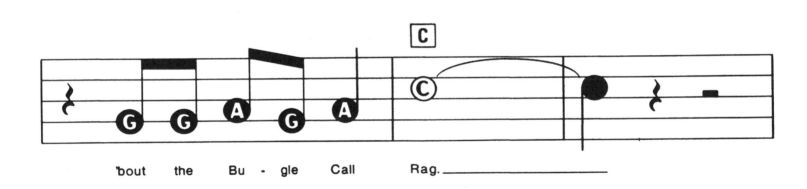

'bout   the   Bu - gle   Call   Rag._____

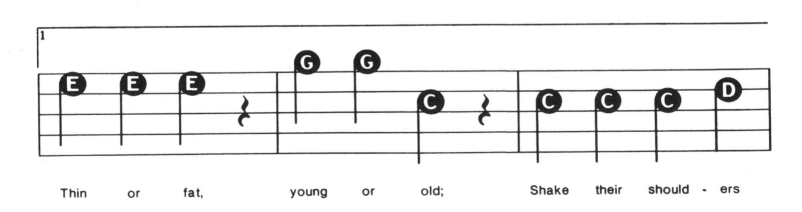

Thin   or   fat,   young   or   old;   Shake   their   should - ers

A Good Man Is Hard To Find

Registration 9
Rhythm: Ballad or Fox Trot

By Eddie Green

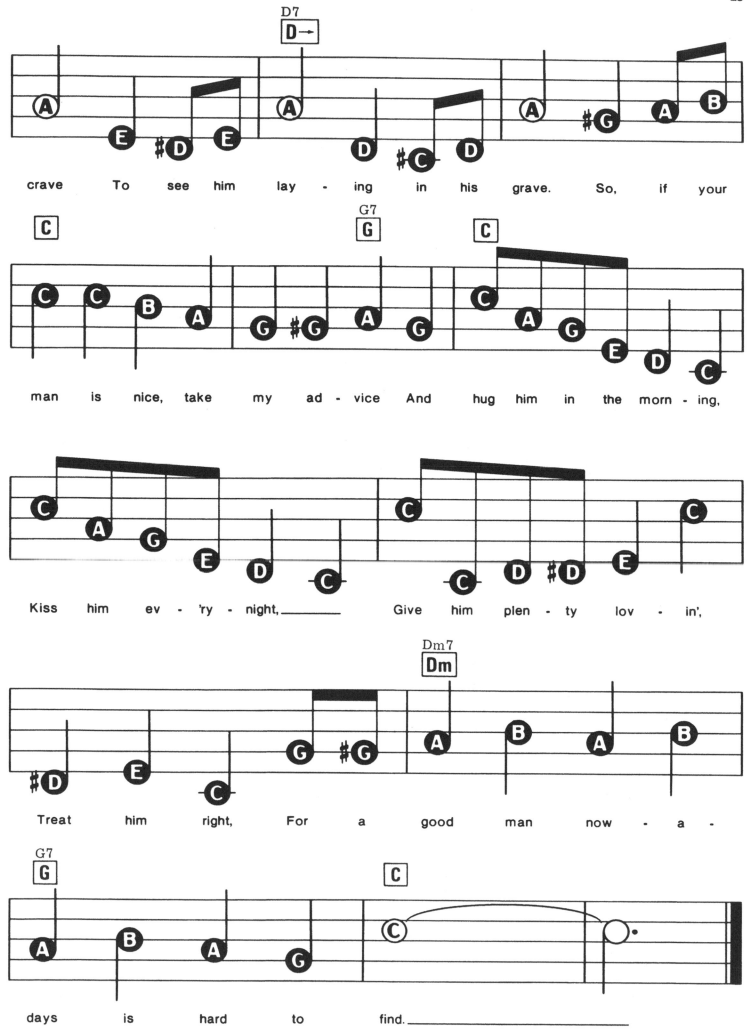

Weary Blues

Registration 2
Rhythm: Ballad or Fox Trot

Lyric by Mort Greene
and George Cates
Music by Artie Matthews

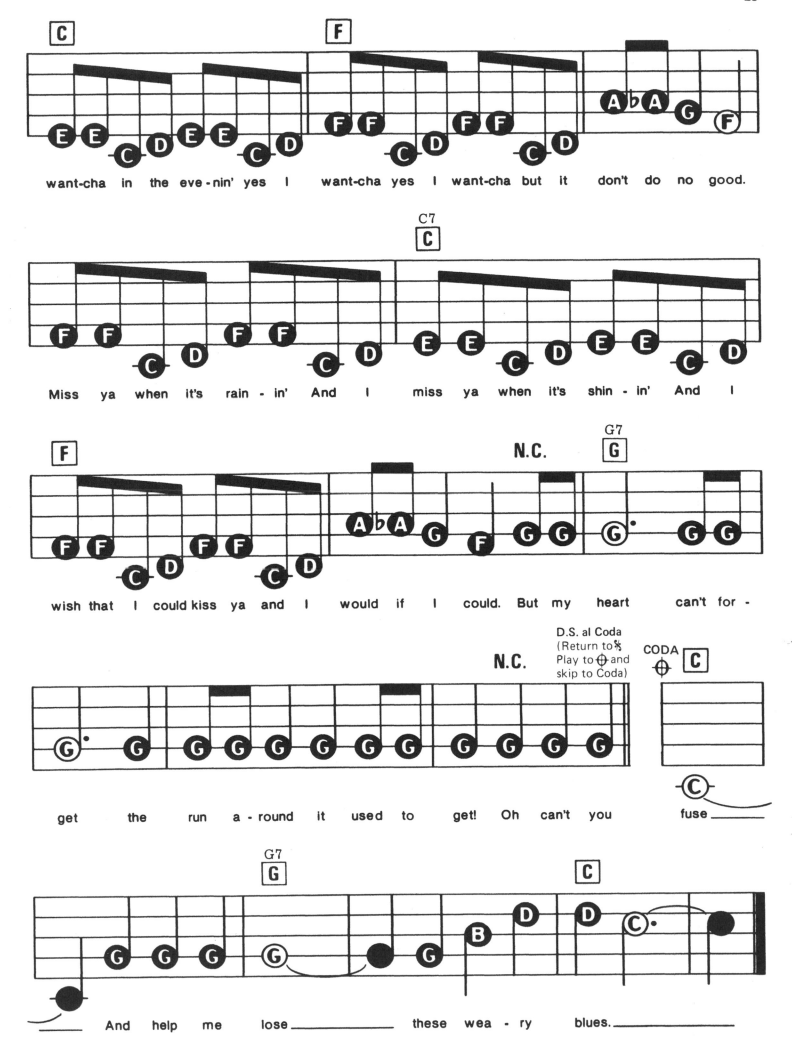

The Entertainer

Registration 8
Rhythm: Swing or Fox Trot

By Scott Joplin

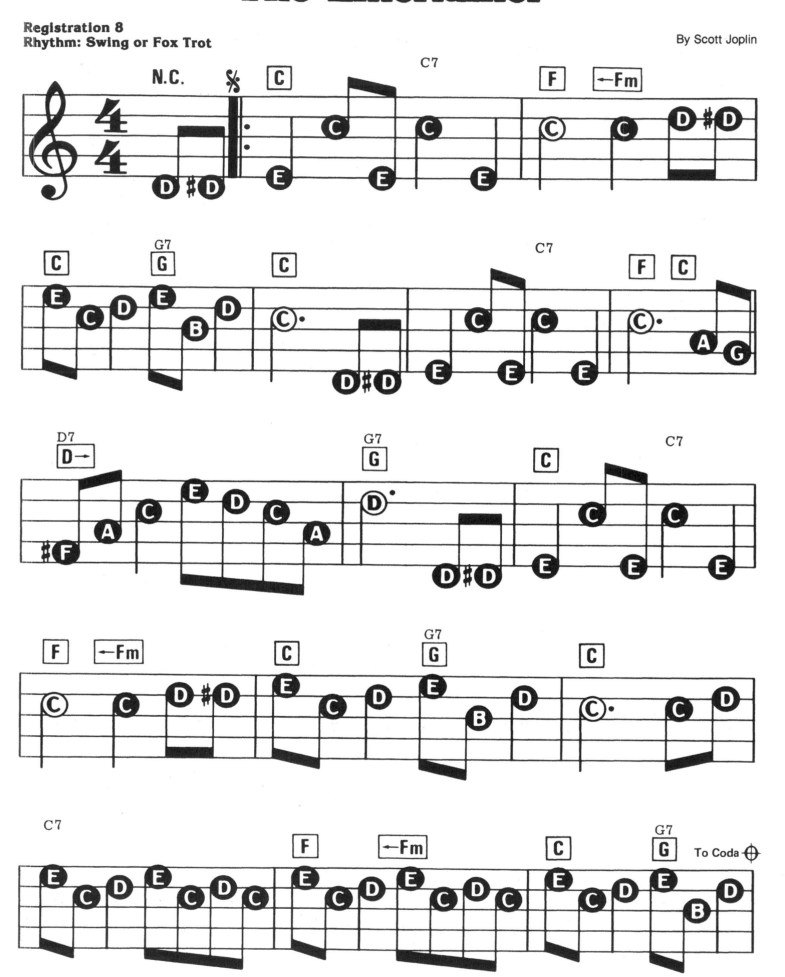

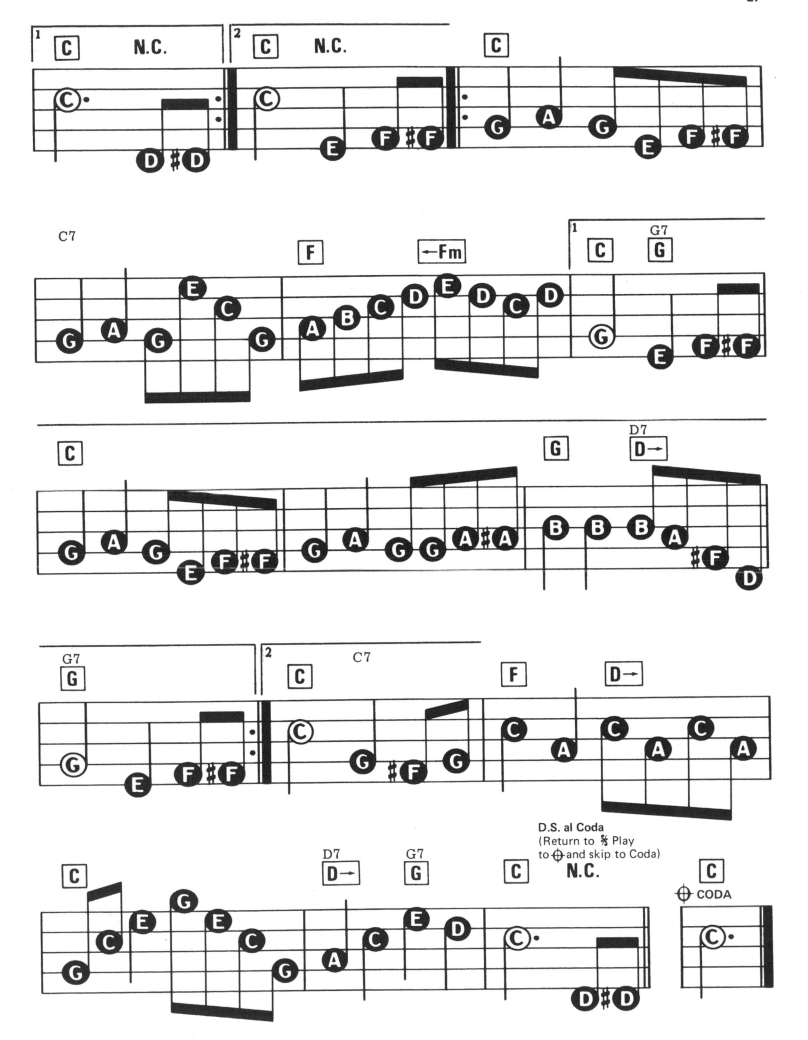

King Porter Stomp

Registration 3
Rhythm: Swing or Fox Trot

By Ferd "Jelly Roll" Morton

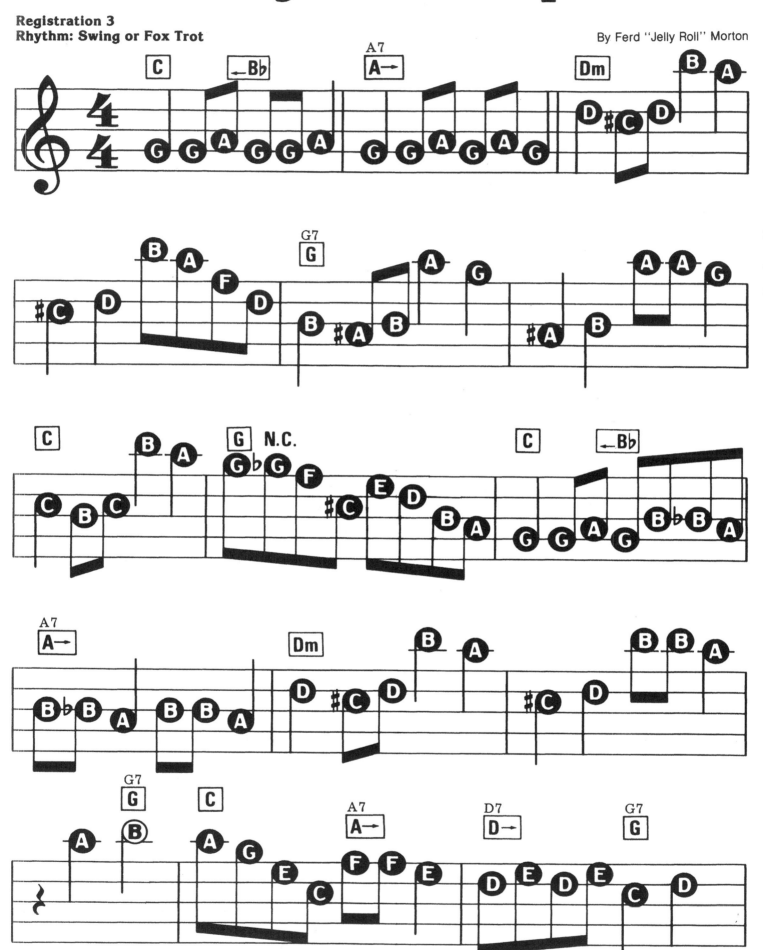

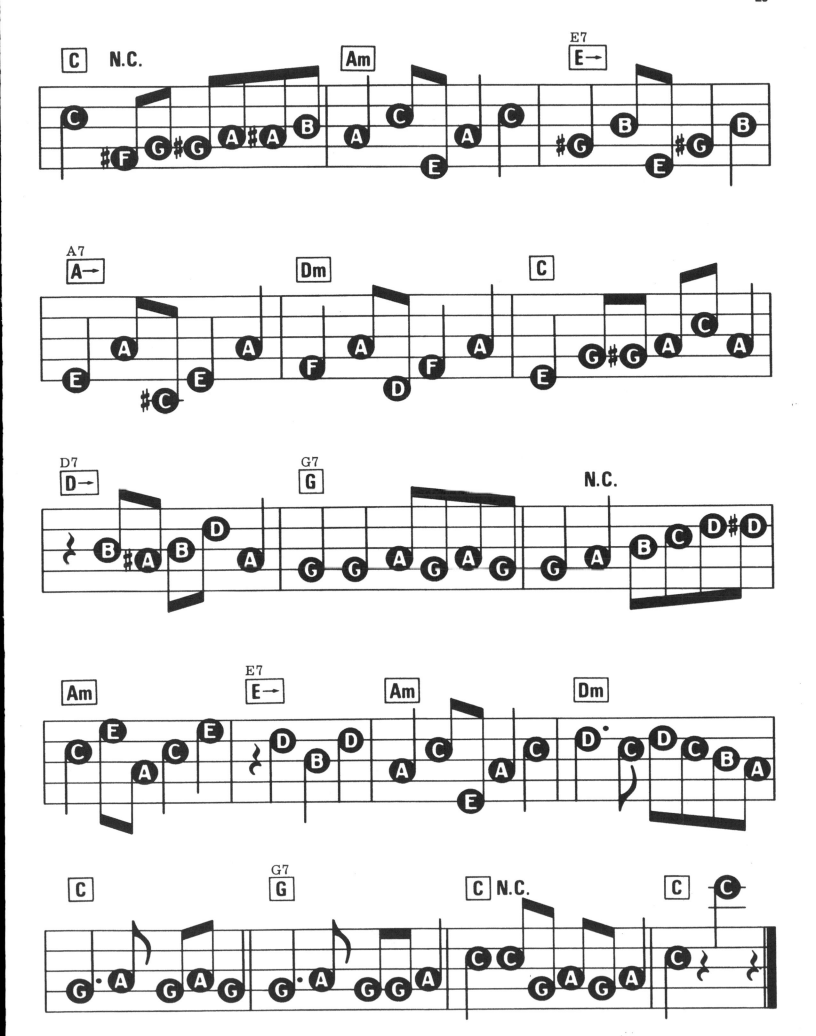

Sugar Foot Stomp

Registration 2
Rhythm: Ballad or Fox Trot

Lyric by Walter Melrose
Music by Joe Oliver

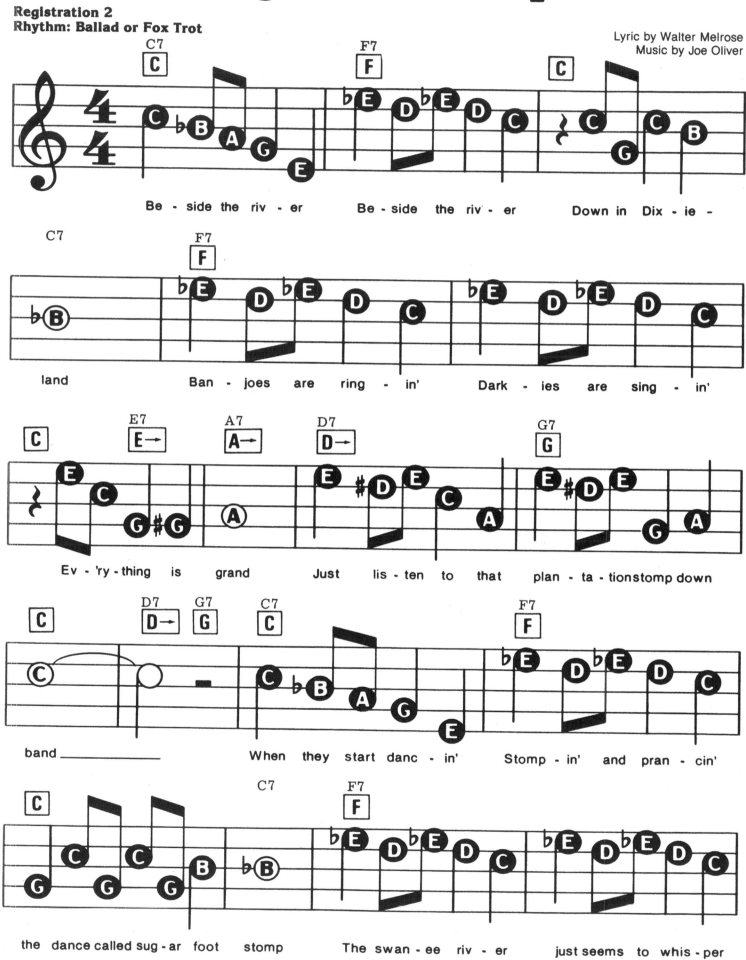

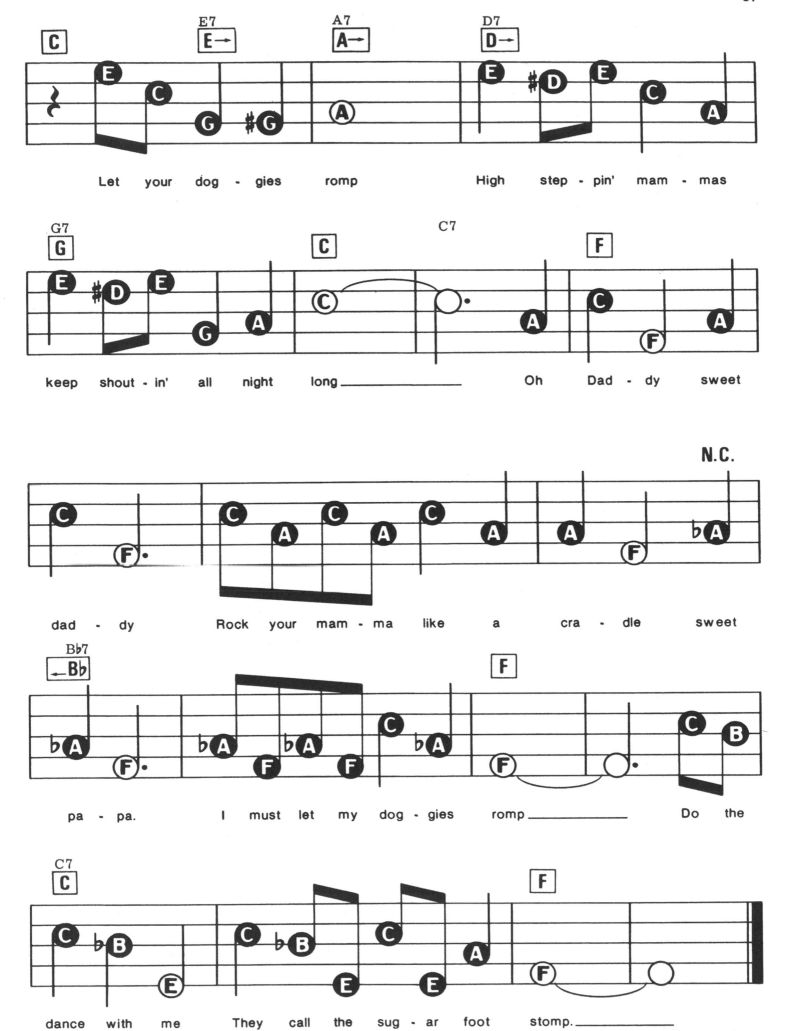

Ivory Rag

Registration 8
Rhythm: Swing or Fox Trot

By Jack Elliott and Lou Busch

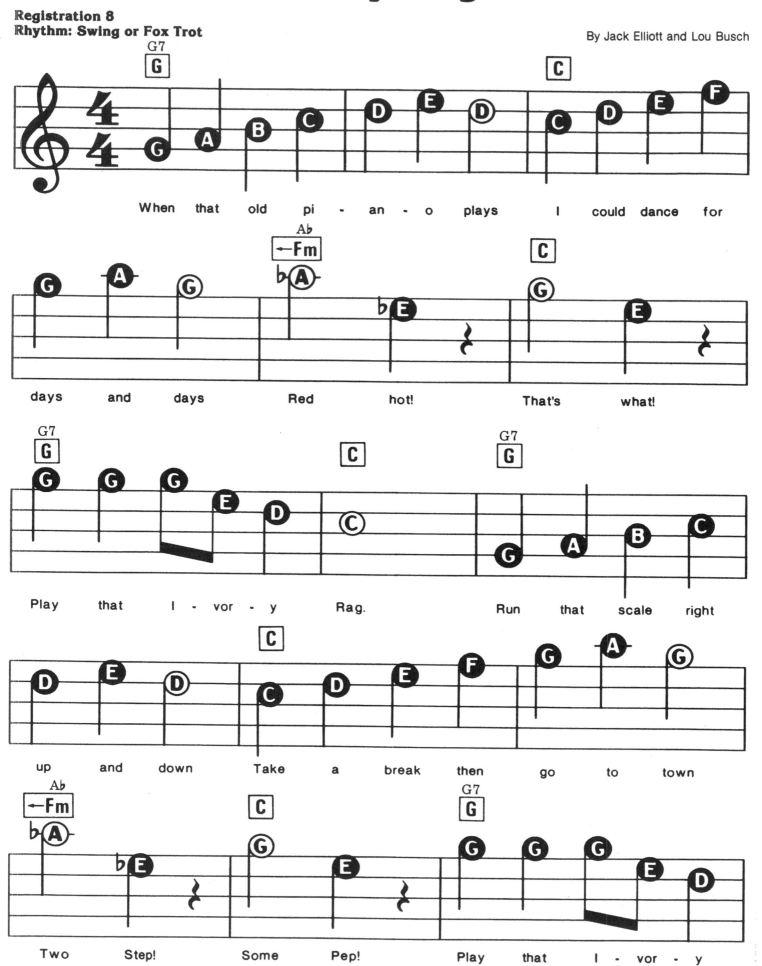

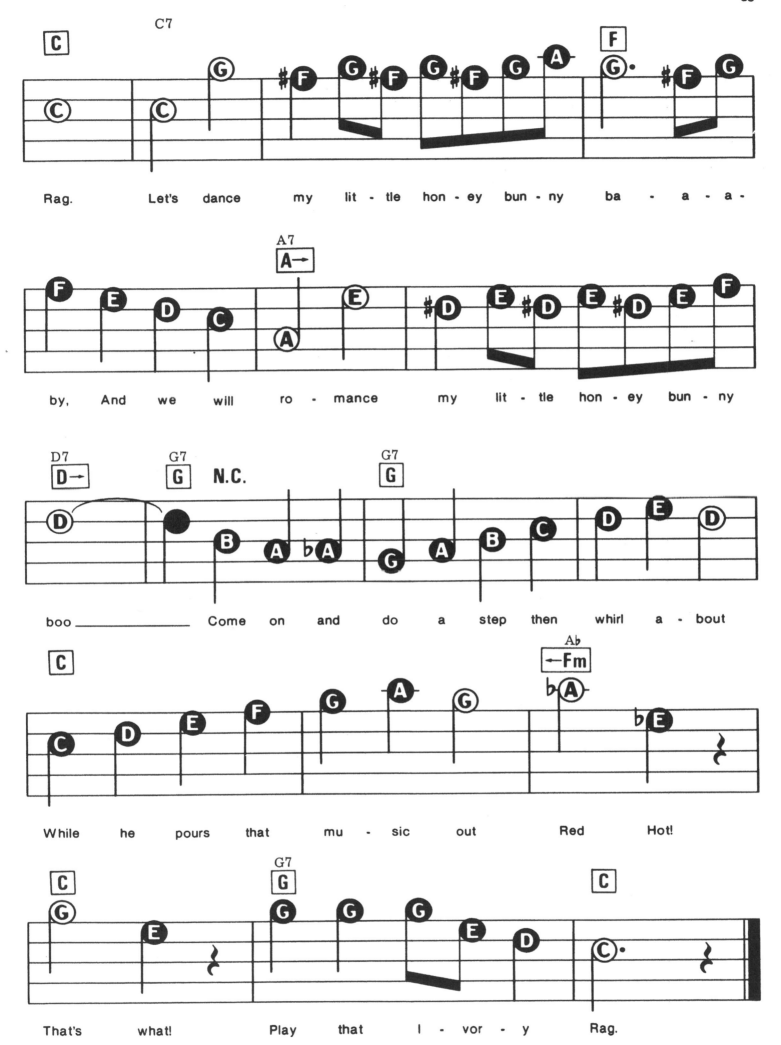

The Man That Got Away

Registration 1
Rhythm: Swing or Fox Trot

Lyric by Ira Gershwin
Music by Harold Arlen

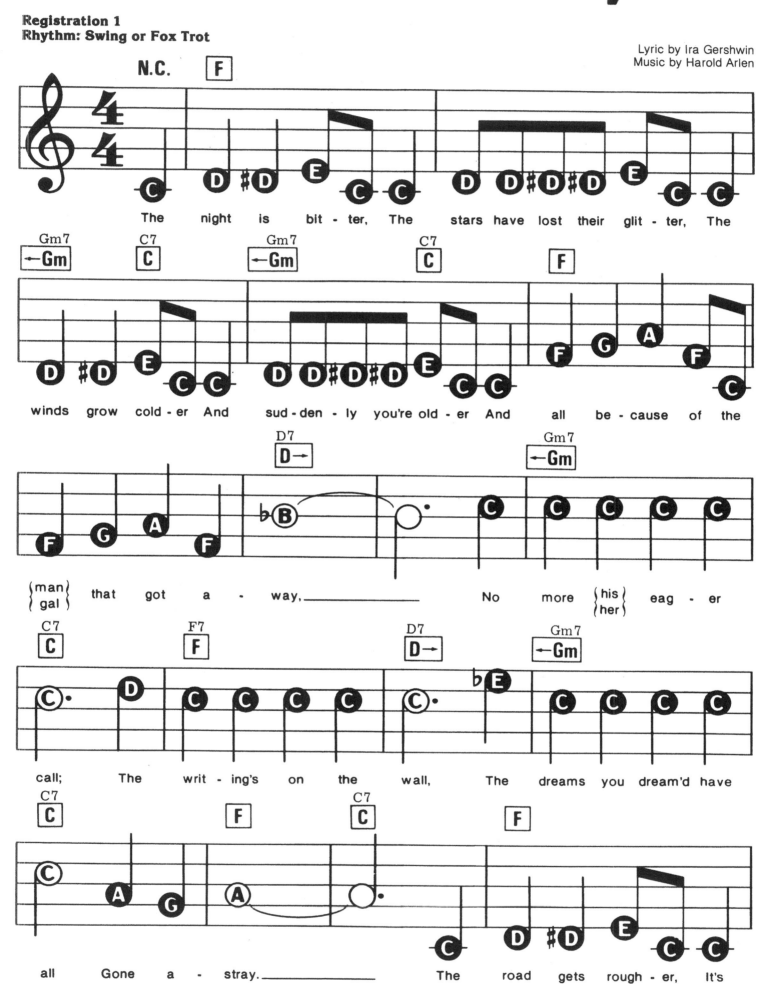

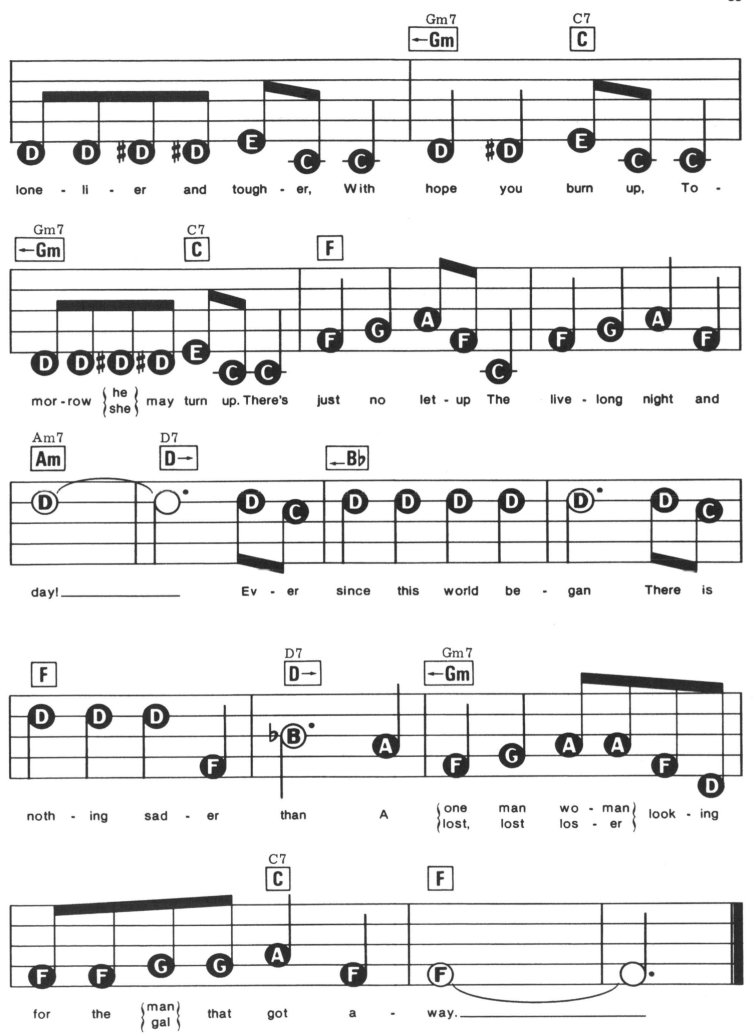

Pine Top's Boogie

Registration 4
Rhythm: Swing or Fox Trot

Lyric by Norman Gimbel
Music by Clarence "Pine Top" Smith

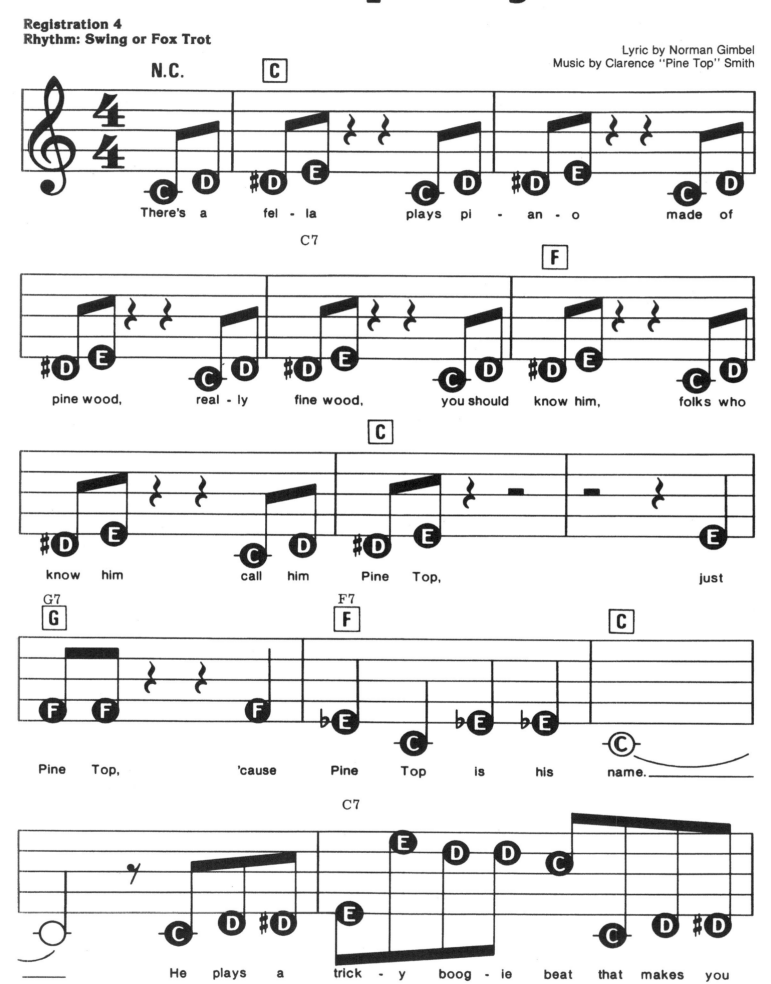

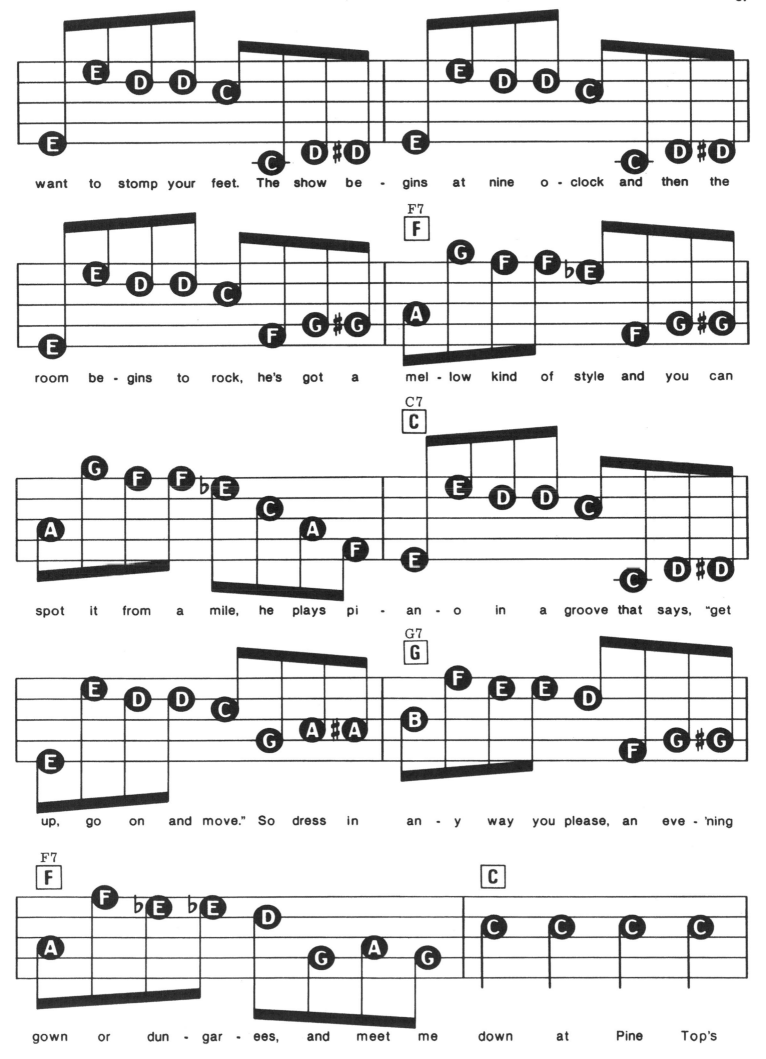

want to stomp your feet. The show be - gins at nine o - clock and then the

room be - gins to rock, he's got a mel - low kind of style and you can

spot it from a mile, he plays pi - an - o in a groove that says, "get

up, go on and move." So dress in an - y way you please, an eve - 'ning

gown or dun - gar - ees, and meet me down at Pine Top's

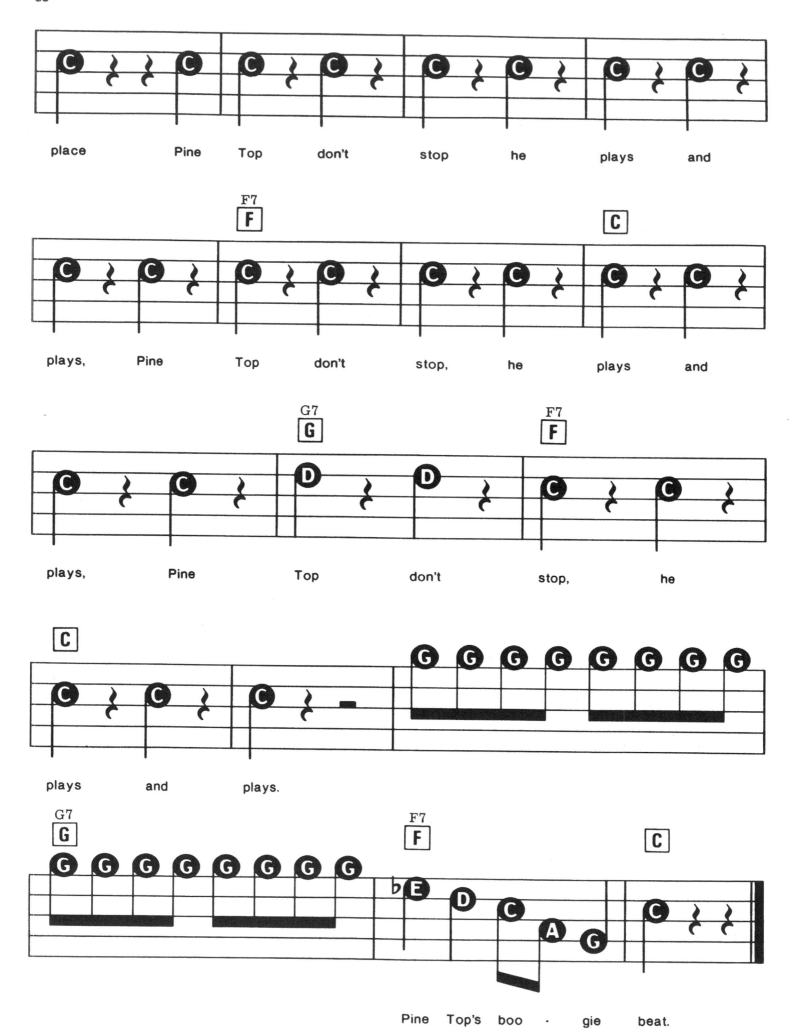

Maple Leaf Rag

Music by Scott Joplin
Revised Music and Lyric by Jule Styne
and Bob Russell

Registration 8
Rhythm: Ballad or Fox Trot

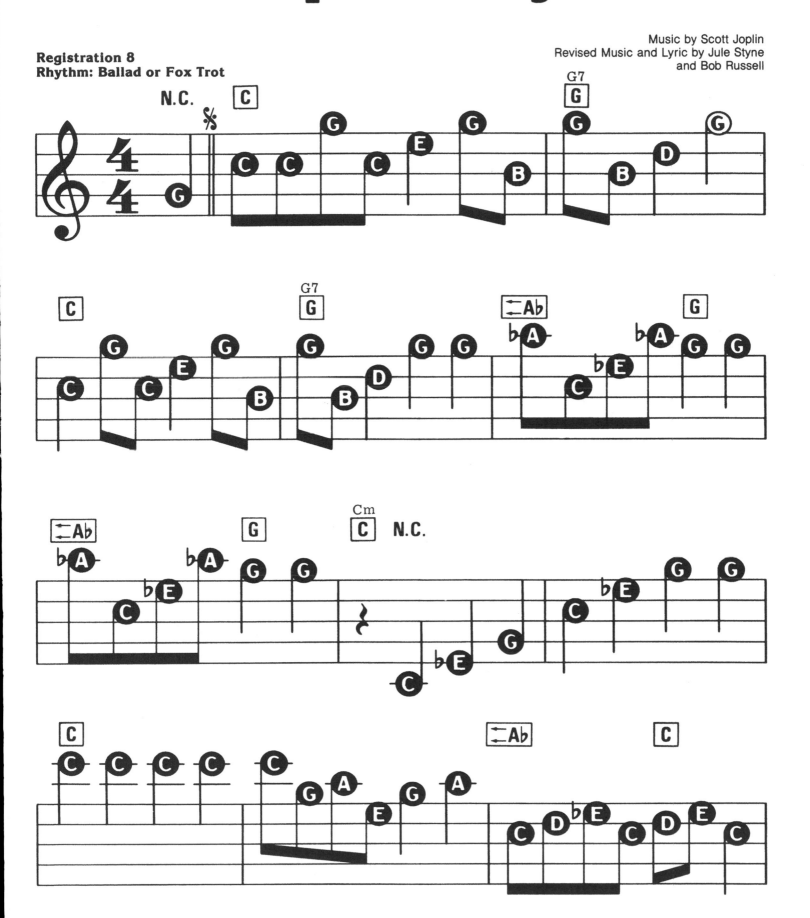

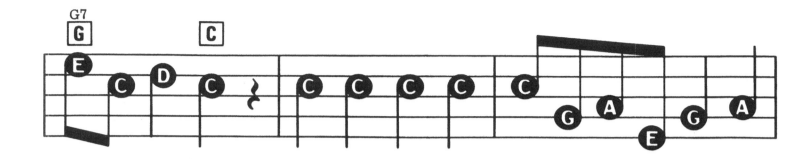

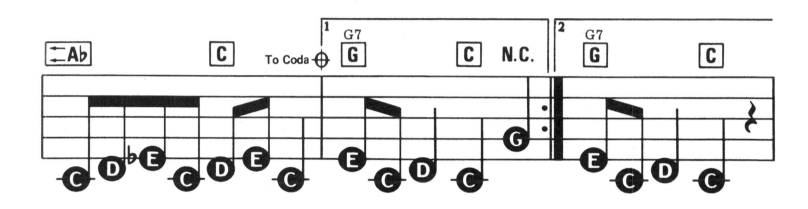

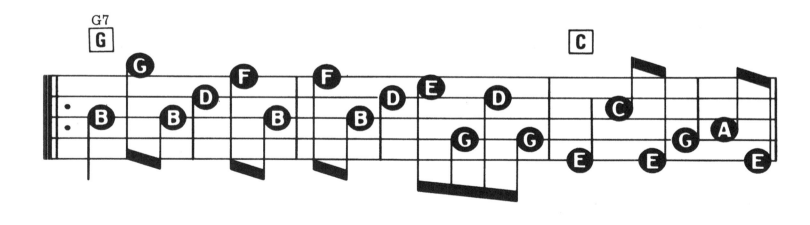

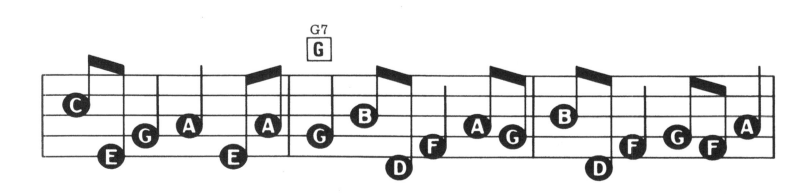

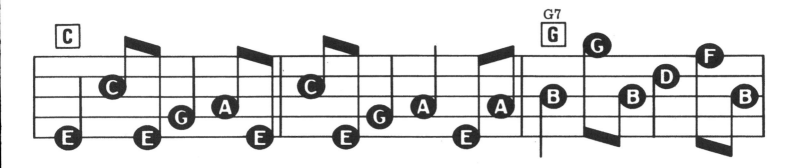

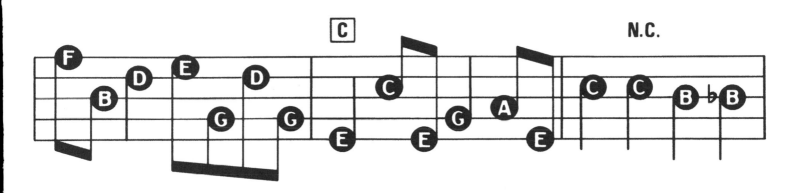

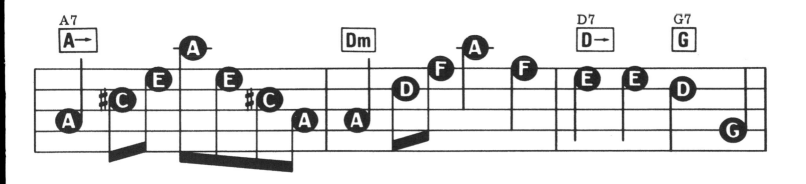

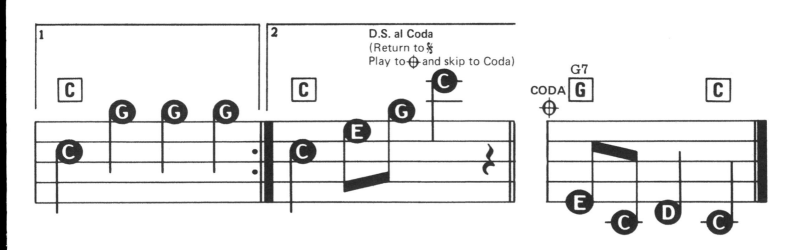

Do You Know What It Means To Miss New Orleans

Registration 7
Rhythm: Ballad or Fox Trot

Lyric by Eddie De Lange
Music by Louis Alter

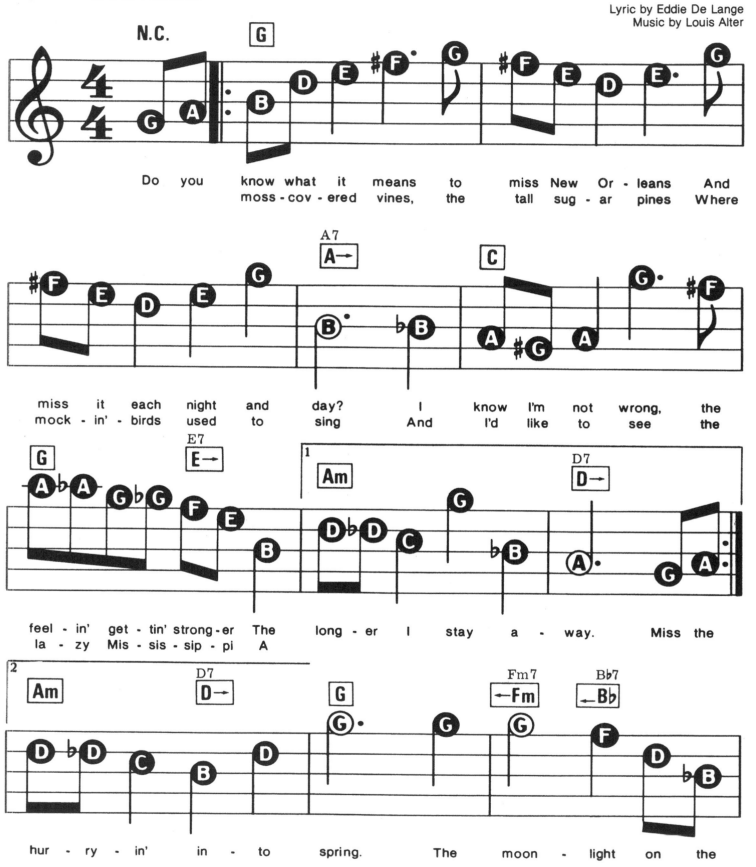

Music Basics

THE MELODY (Right Hand)

The melody of a song appears as large lettered notes on a staff. The letter name corresponds to a key on the keyboard of an organ.

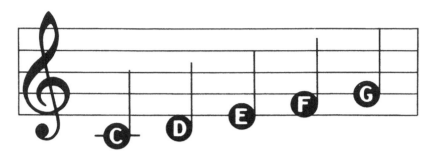

ACCOMPANIMENT (Left Hand)

The arrangements in this series have been written for all types of chord accompaniment.

1 One button (chord organ) or one-key chords.

2 Three-note (triad) chords.

3 Conventional, or standard chord positions.

Chord names, called chord symbols, appear above the melody line as either a boxed symbol $\boxed{\text{C}}$

or as an alternate chord (**C7**)

or both $\begin{array}{c}\text{C7}\\\boxed{\text{C}}\end{array}$

1 For chord organ or one-key chords, play whichever chord name is on your unit.

2 If you are playing triad chords, follow the boxed symbols. A triad chord is played like this:

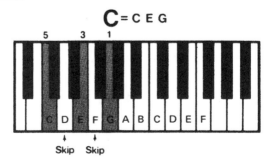

- Place your little finger on the key which has the same letter name as the chord.

- Skip a white key and place your middle finger on the next white key.

- Skip another white key and place your thumb on the next white key.

In some cases, there is an ARROW to the **left** or to the **right** of the chord name.

The arrow indicates moving one of the triad notes either to the **left** or to the **right** on the keyboard.

To understand this, first think of a chord symbol as having three sections, representing the three notes of the chord.

An ARROW is positioned next to the chord letter in one of these sections, indicating which of the three notes to change. For example:

• An arrow to the left means to move a note of the chord **down** (left) to the next adjacent key.

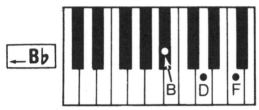

In this example where the arrow is in the **lower left**, or "1" position, move the first note "B" **down** to the black key B♭.

• An arrow to the right means to move a note of the chord **up** (right) to the next adjacent key.

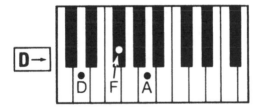

In this example where the arrow is in the **middle**, or "2" position, move the middle note **up** to the black key F♯.

3 If you are playing standard chord positions, play the chord in the boxed symbol, unless an alternate chord is indicated. Play alternate chords whenever possible.

For your reference, a Chord Speller Chart of standard chord positions appears in the back of this book.

REGISTRATION AND RHYTHM

A Registration number is shown above the music for each song. This number corresponds to the same number on the Registration Guide which appears on the inside front cover of this book. The Registration numbers also correspond to the numbers on the E-Z Play TODAY Registration Guides that are available for many brands of organs. See your organ dealer for the details.

You may wish to select your own favorite registration or perhaps experiment with different voice combinations. Then add an automatic rhythm. . . and HAVE FUN.

Guitar Chord Chart

To use the E-Z Play TODAY Guitar Chord chart, simply find the **letter name** of the chord at the top of the chart, and the **kind of chord** (Major, Minor, etc.) in the column at the left. Read down and across to find the correct chord. Suggested fingering has been indicated, but feel free to use alternate fingering.

	C	Db	D	Eb	E	F
MAJOR						
MINOR (m)						
7TH (7)						
MINOR 7TH (m7)						

	F♯	G	A♭	A	B♭	B
MAJOR	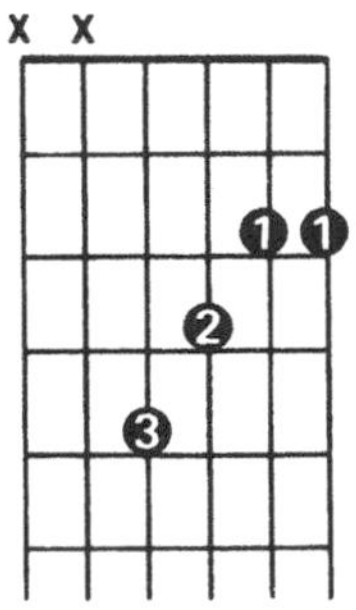	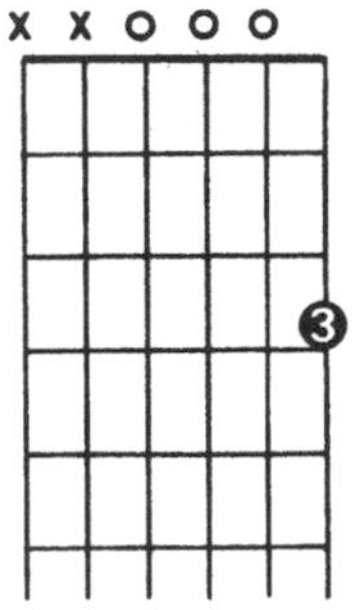	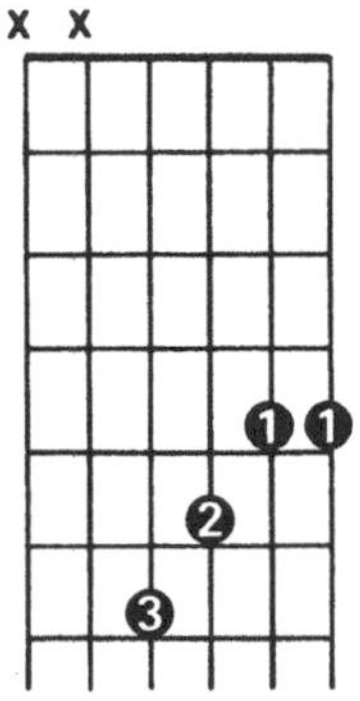	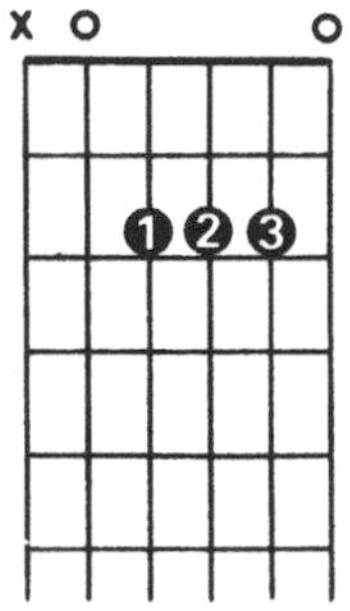	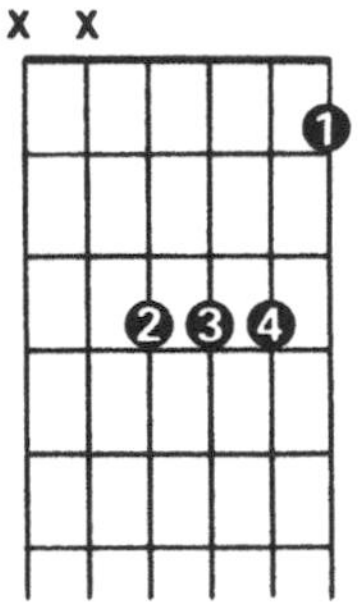	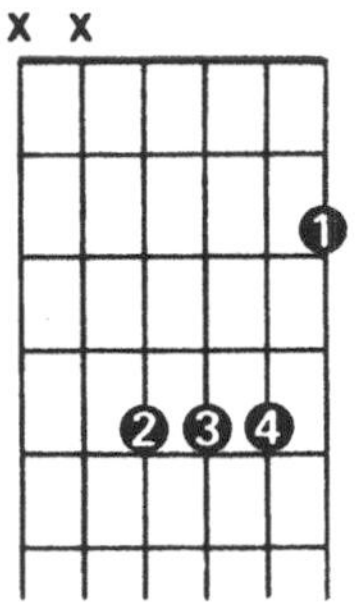
MINOR (m)	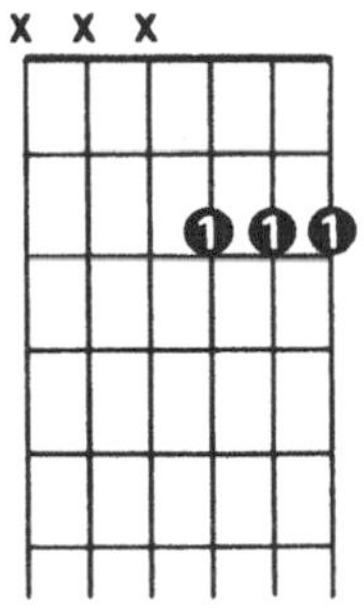	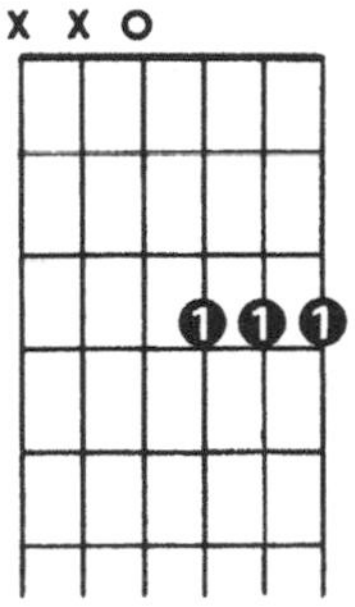	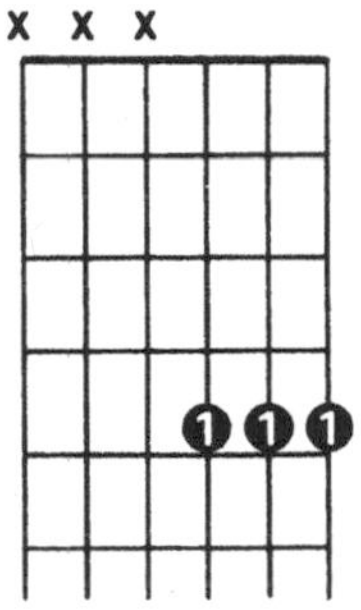	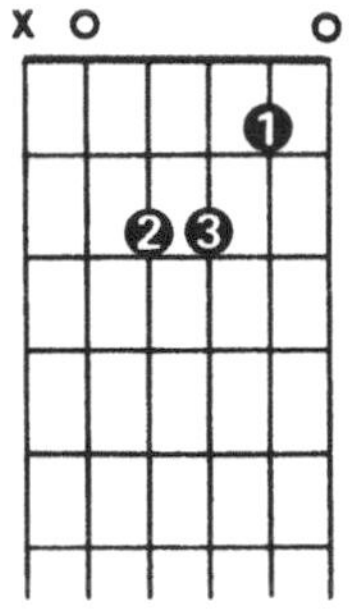	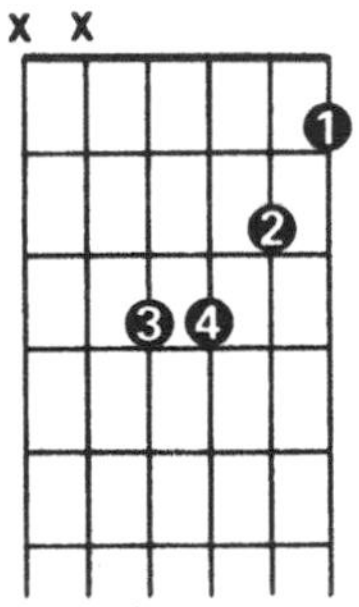	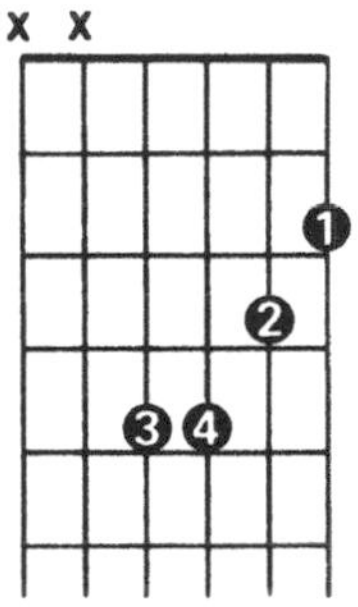
7TH (7)	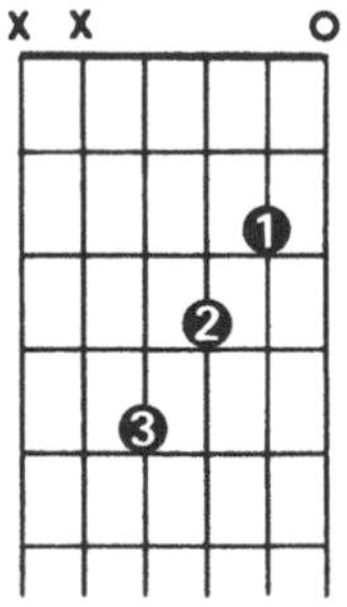	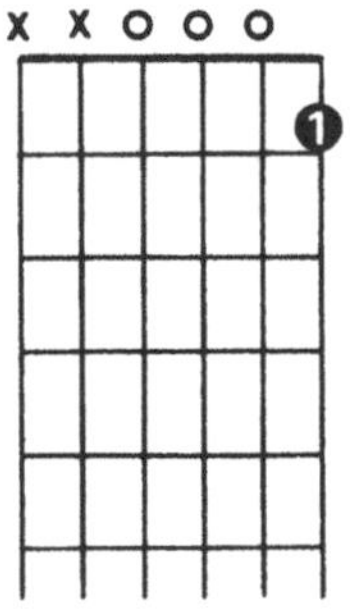	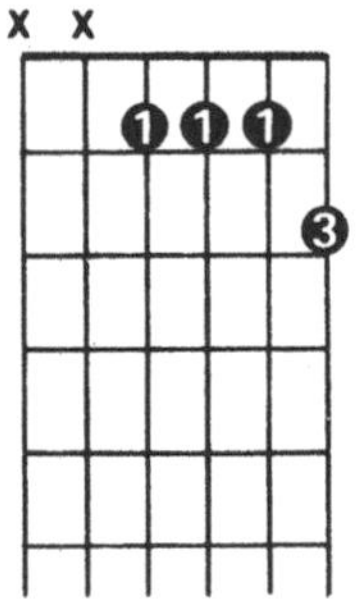	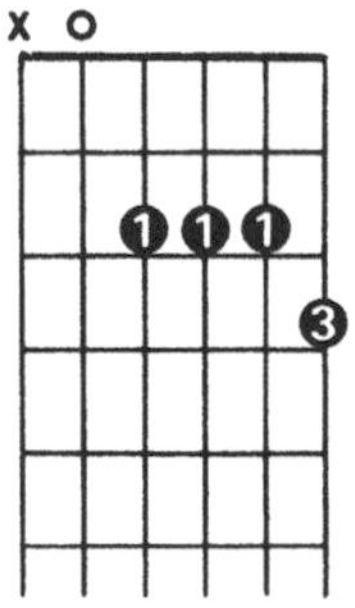	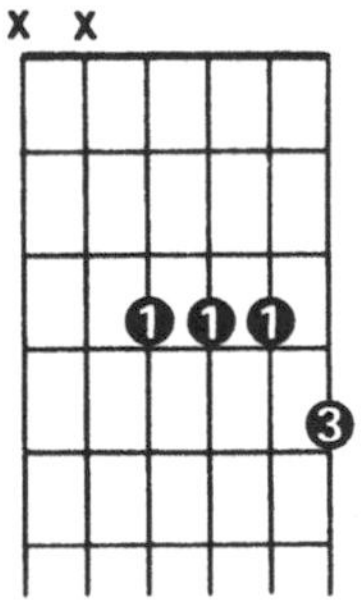	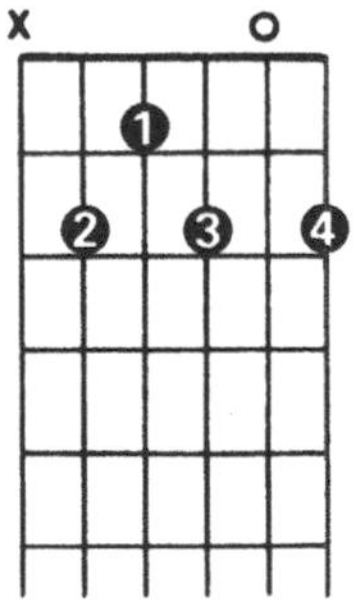
MINOR 7TH (m7)	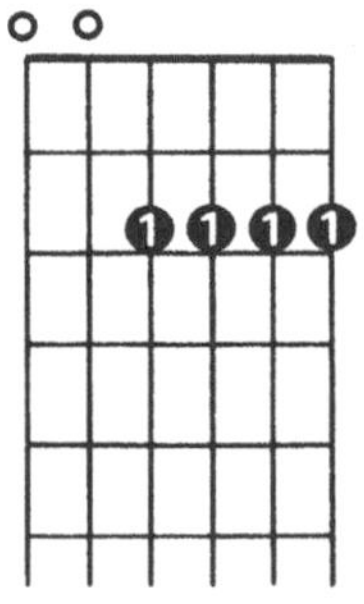	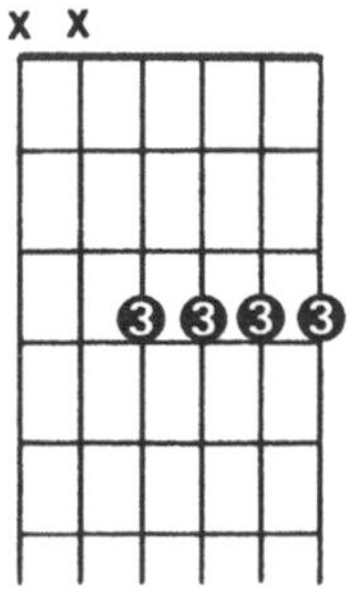	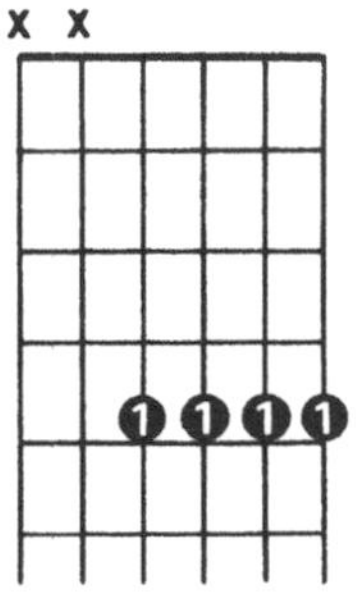	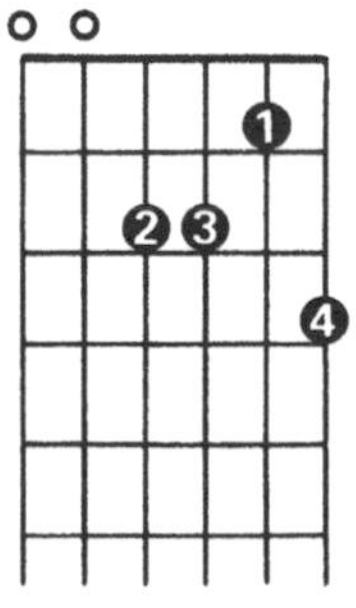	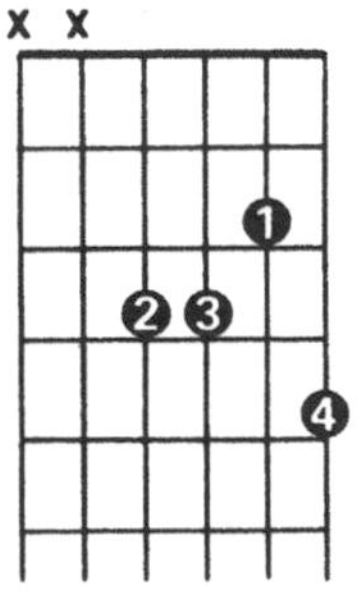	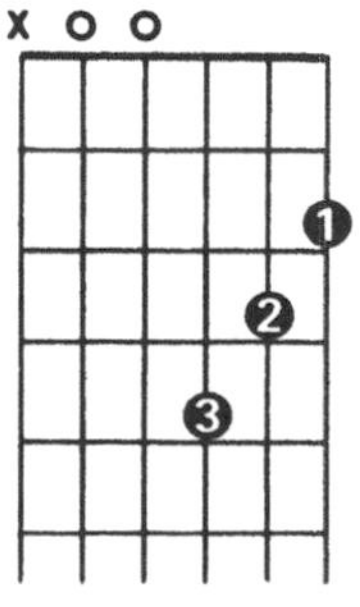

Chord Speller Chart
of Standard Chord Positions

For those who play standard chord positions, all chords used in the E-Z Play TODAY music arrangements are shown here in their most commonly used chord positions. Suggested fingering is also indicated, but feel free to use alternate fingering.

CHORD FAMILY Abbrev.	MAJOR	MINOR (m)	7TH (7)	MINOR 7TH (m7)
C	5 2 1 G-C-E	5 2 1 G-C-Eb	5 3 2 1 G-Bb-C-E	5 3 2 1 G-Bb-C-Eb
Db	5 2 1 Ab-Db-F	5 2 1 Ab-Db-E	5 3 2 1 Ab-B-Db-F	5 3 2 1 Ab-B-Db-E
D	5 3 1 F#-A-D	5 2 1 A-D-F	5 3 2 1 F#-A-C-D	5 3 2 1 A-C-D-F
Eb	5 3 1 G-Bb-Eb	5 3 1 Gb-Bb-Eb	5 3 2 1 G-Bb-Db-Eb	5 3 2 1 Gb-Bb-Db-Eb
E	5 3 1 G#-B-E	5 3 1 G-B-E	5 3 2 1 G#-B-D-E	5 3 2 1 G-B-D-E
F	4 2 1 A-C-F	4 2 1 Ab-C-F	5 3 2 1 A-C-Eb-F	5 3 2 1 Ab-C-Eb-F
F#	4 2 1 F#-A#-C#	4 2 1 F#-A-C#	5 3 2 1 F#-A#-C#-E	5 3 2 1 F#-A-C#-E
G	5 3 1 G-B-D	5 3 1 G-Bb-D	5 3 2 1 G-B-D-F	5 3 2 1 G-Bb-D-F
Ab	4 2 1 Ab-C-Eb	4 2 1 Ab-B-Eb	5 3 2 1 Ab-C-Eb-Gb	5 3 2 1 Ab-B-Eb-Gb
A	4 2 1 A-C#-E	4 2 1 A-C-E	5 4 2 1 G-A-C#-E	5 4 2 1 G-A-C-E
Bb	4 2 1 Bb-D-F	4 2 1 Bb-Db-F	5 4 2 1 Ab-Bb-D-F	5 4 2 1 Ab-Bb-Db-F
B	5 2 1 F#-B-D#	5 2 1 F#-B-D	5 3 2 1 F#-A-B-D#	5 3 2 1 F#-A-B-D